Getting Understanding

Developing a Life on the Teachings of the Bible

by Peggy Musgrove

Table of Contents

Introduction

In my previous books, you—my readers—and I have walked through God's Word. First, we were *Gathering Wisdom* as we walked through the Bible, gleaning a thought from each book, as we would pick a flower while walking through a garden. Our goal was to become acquainted with God's Word so we could return often.

In the second book, we were *Gaining Knowledge*, specifically knowledge of God. Our goal was to know God as He is presented in the Bible; to know the true God, not a product of our imagination.

Then we ask ourselves, "What is the next logical step in our study of God's Word?" Solomon gives some advice in Proverbs 4:7: "Acquire wisdom; and with all your acquiring, get understanding."

Getting Understanding of the Scriptures will be our goal for this book.

Defining terms is a beginning step in getting understanding. We will ask three questions to define the correlation of wisdom, knowledge and understanding. We could ask first, "What does the Bible say?" The answers to that question give us Bible knowledge.

Then we could ask, "What does the Bible mean?" Based on the knowledge we gained, we answer the second question. Wisdom has been defined as applied knowledge.

We ask further, "What does the Bible mean to me?" When I appropriate the factual knowledge of the Bible, wisely interpreting the meaning, I understand how to apply the principles to my life. That is getting understanding.

Our approach will be different from other books. We will move from reading the Bible chronologically to reading it thematically. John 3:16 has been called the "theme verse" of the Bible:

> For God so loved the world, that He gave His only begotten Son, that whoever believes in Him shall not perish, but have eternal life.

Our quest will be to know God's Son, to understand His teaching and to apply it to our lives.

Peggy Musgrove

Dedication

To my three grandchildren,
Colin, Christopher, and **Grace,**
and to the generations to come,
with the sincere desire that they have lifelong
communication with God
through their knowlege of His Word.

Acknowledgements

This book would not have been completed without the help
of my daughters, **Darla** and **Diane**, and their husbands,
Rick Knoth and **David Awbrey**. All are professionals in the field of publication.

My late husband **Derald Musgrove**, who always had a camera with him
to preserve the beauty of nature, took all the floral photographs.

So this book is a family project.

We also extend great appreciation to Steve Lopez for designing
the left-hand graphics pages.

For no man can lay
a foundation
other than the one
which is laid,
which is Jesus Christ.

1 Corinthians 3:11

A Firm Foundation

*H*ave you seen a child eagerly tear open a gift to see what was inside? That is similar to what we are doing with this study. John 3:16 says that God gave us a gift—His Son—that we might have eternal life. For this study, we will "open the package" to learn about God's gift to us.

Matthew records one of Jesus' first teaching sessions, commonly called the Sermon on the Mount. He had just begun His ministry; large crowds were following Him from Judea and beyond the Jordan River.

Jesus concludes His sermon by saying there are two possible responses to His teaching. His hearers could respond either positively or negatively—a statement that acknowledges the power God gives to each of us. The choice would be revealed—not by applauding His teaching but by their actions following His teaching.

Jesus compared the choices to building a house "on a rock" or "on the sand." The house on a rock would not fall during a storm but the other one would be destroyed. He was illustrating how choices affect our lives.

The apostle Paul picks up the comparison of the believer's life to a building in 1 Corinthians 3:10-11:

> But each man must be careful how he builds on it. For no man can lay a foundation other than the one which is laid, which is Jesus Christ.

Just as a building needs a solid foundation, so does our life. Jesus Christ, God's gift to us, offers a solid foundation. If we want a great life, we start with a great foundation and then we are careful how we build on it. Our choices and our actions determine the end result.

Prayer: Lord, help us see the importance of building our lives on a firm foundation. Thank You for being that foundation and our Guide as we build on it.

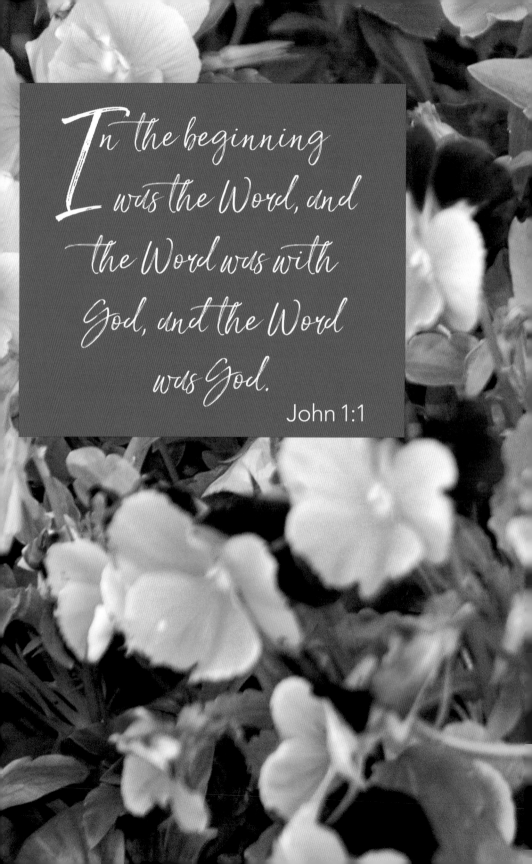

Christ, the Living Word

*T*he proposed size of the building determines the size of the foundation. Designers consider not only the breadth and height of a building, but also the depth of the foundation. Likewise, the strength of our spiritual journey comes from the depth of our relationship with Christ.

In the opening of his gospel, John includes many names and attributes for Jesus. He concludes his writing about Jesus' life with this statement:

> And there are also many other things which Jesus did, which if they were written in detail, I suppose that even the world itself would not contain the books that would be written. (21:25)

If John, who walked closely with Jesus, felt that way, then we can learn about Jesus. We will focus on Jesus' names and attributes for a few weeks. We want to know the strength of the foundation on which we are building our lives.

John opens his gospel with these words:

> In the beginning was the Word, and the Word was with God, and the Word was God. (1:1)

Here John tells us Jesus was divine, and present with God in the beginning. His words remind us of Genesis: "In the beginning God. . . ." Being with God is a good place to start anything—our days, our projects and our lives.

The first title John gives Jesus is "the Word," which scholars sometimes refer to as the "Living Word." By using this title, John was saying Jesus' entire life was an expression of the character of God, as our words are expressions of our character. What a challenge for us as we follow Jesus' example, so that everything we do is a consistent expression of the Word of God.

Prayer: *Lord, we know people are changed more by what we do than what we say. Help us to be living examples of Your Word.*

I came that they may have

life,

and have it abundantly.

John 10:10

Christ, the Life

*E*ternal life is promised to the believer in what we call the theme verse of the Bible: "whoever believes in Him shall not perish, but have eternal life" (John 3:16).

John introduced Christ as the source of life, saying, "in Him was life" (1:4). Eternal life is clearly the destiny of the believer. However, in the Book of John we read that Christ's life abides in us now, enriching our earthly life.

Jesus said: "The thief comes only to . . . destroy; I came that they may have life, and have it abundantly" (John 10:10). The word "abundant" indicates fullness or plenty; hence, an abundant life will have more than an ordinary life.

Some would have us believe abundance indicates health, wealth and prosperity; that only good things will happen to us. The absence of health and wealth means lack of faith or sin in our lives. If we take this position, we have no means of dealing with hard issues of life.

Abundance means far more than having material comfort. Because Christians always have the presence of God, they will always have "more than enough" to cope with any situation. Paul wrote Philippians 4:12,13:

> In any and every circumstance I have learned the secret of being filled and going hungry, both of having abundance and suffering need. I can do all things through Him who strengthens me.

Paul's contentment came from his confidence in Christ, not from the comfort of his circumstances. In any situation, Christ's presence gives peace, with the added joy of knowing we will spend eternity with Him.

This is abundant living.

Prayer: *Lord, our hearts abound with gratitude for we know You are walking with us in every situation. Thank You for the peace and joy Your presence brings.*

In *Him* was *life*; and the life was the *Light of men.*

John 1:4

Christ, the Light

Words describing Jesus come tumbling out as John begins his gospel. He says Jesus, the divine eternal Creator, is the source of life, the embodied Word of God and the Light of all humanity—and all that in just five verses.

Introducing Jesus as the Light of the World, John says, "In him was life; and the life was the light of men" (1:4). This verse suggests the universality of Jesus' coming; He came not only for the Jews but also for all humanity. John repeats the universality theme when he says that "whosoever" comes to Jesus in believing faith will have eternal life (3:16).

Nothing can keep natural light from shining, making it an appropriate comparative term describing Jesus' life. Romans 1 tells us the universal knowledge of God is available to all humanity, in verse 20:

> For since the creation of the world His invisible attributes, His eternal power and divine nature, have been clearly seen, being understood through what has been made, so that they are without excuse.

Unfortunately, people still refuse to believe the obvious, closing their eyes to spiritual light and life.

John the Baptist bore witness about the Light, but the majority rejected his witness. Much later, Jesus said that judgment would come to those who loved darkness rather than the light.

In contrast, those who practice truth would come to Christ, the Light, and benefit from the relationship with Him, as all living things grow when they have appropriate light. This teaching shows the two ways to respond to Christ: We can come to the Light, or shut it out. The choice is ours.

Prayer: *Lord, help us to choose the pathway of Light—to walk in Light as You are in the Light and enjoy Your fellowship here, and ultimately in our eternal home.*

Christ, the Lamb

John the Baptist, in his first message, said someone greater than he would come after him. When Jesus appeared, John boldly declared: "Behold the Lamb of God who takes away the sins of the world" (John 1:29).

That statement would have intrigued the Jewish crowd. Lambs were sacrificed annually at Passover. Lambs had been included in their worship since Abraham offered a lamb for his son Isaac. Before deliverance from Egypt, each family sacrificed a lamb.

They were familiar with lambs being offered for a man, for a family and for the nation. But John the Baptist called this person a Lamb for the world, a direct reference to Jesus' death as the atoning sacrifice for the entire world.

The apostle John picks up the theme of Christ as the Lamb of God in the Book of Revelation. He has a vision of the Lamb on the throne, before an innumerable multitude whose robes were made white by the blood of the Lamb (Revelation 7:14). He describes the saints singing "the song of Moses . . . and the Lamb" (15:3) and the blessing of those called to "the marriage supper of the Lamb" (19:9).

John says the Lamb also shows His wrath at ungodliness, so much that people cried to the mountains for relief: "Hide us from the . . . wrath of the Lamb" (6:16).

Near the end of Revelation, John gives this hopeful prophecy:

> There will no longer be any curse; and the throne of God and of the Lamb will be in it, and his bond-servants will serve him. (22:3)

As the Lamb of God, Jesus died for our sins. When we accept Him as Savior, we look forward to eternity and singing the song of Moses and the Lamb.

Prayer: Lord, our hearts are filled with gratitude for Your atoning work, and with anticipation for the day we will see You as the Lamb on Your throne.

. . . so that at the *name of Jesus* every knee will bow . . . and that *every tongue will confess that Jesus Christ is Lord,* to the glory of God the Father.

Philippians 2:10,11

Christ, the Lord

*W*hen John the Baptist appeared in the wilderness calling people to repentance, he quoted Isaiah's prophecy: "I am the voice of one crying in the wilderness, 'Make straight the way of the Lord'" (John 1:23). He was referring to the common practice of a forerunner clearing the way for a prominent person, implying that the coming "Lord" was someone significant.

In the Book of John, the title "Lord" is often used to refer to Jesus. The multitudes call Jesus "Lord" after the feeding of the 5,000. When the multitudes leave, He questions the disciples' loyalty. Peter responds: "Lord, to whom shall we go? You have words of eternal life" (John 6:68).

Some who had no previous contact with Jesus use this title of "Lord." For example, the woman taken in adultery calls Him "Lord" (John 8:11). He demonstrates His authority by forgiving her sins. The blind man, healed by the pool of Siloam, first referred to Him as "the man called Jesus." When questioned by the Pharisees, he calls Him a "prophet," but later when Jesus questions him, his response is "Lord, I believe" (John 9:38).

As we read the last events of Jesus' life, we hear those who are close to Him frequently using the title "Lord." After Lazarus's death, both Martha and Mary say the same thing, "Lord, if You had been here, my brother would not have died" (John 11:21,32). At the Triumphal Entry, the masses cry: "Hosanna! Blessed is He who comes in the name of the Lord" (John 12:13). In the intimacy of the Last Supper, both Peter and John refer to Jesus as "Lord."

Eventually, Scripture teaches, "At the name of Jesus, every knee will bow of those who are in heaven and on earth and under the earth, and that every tongue will confess that Jesus Christ is Lord" (Philippians 2:10,11).

Prayer: Lord, we look forward to that day but every day we also gratefully acknowledge You as Lord of our lives. Amen.

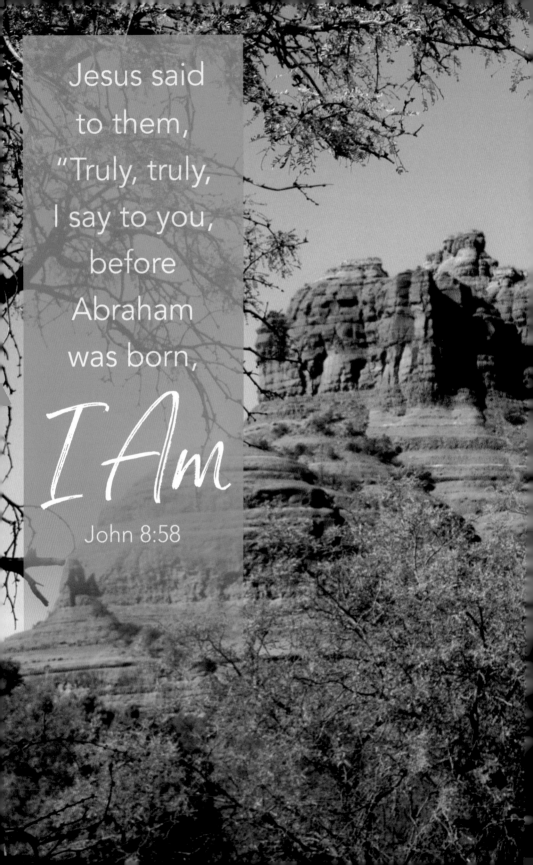

Jesus said to them, "Truly, truly, I say to you, before Abraham was born, *I Am*

John 8:58

Christ, the Great I AM

The contemporary Christian song, "Mary, Did You Know?" closes with the questions:

> "Did you know that your Baby Boy is heaven's perfect Lamb?
> The sleeping Child you're holding is the Great I Am."[1]

The submissiveness of the Lamb seems to be diametrically opposed to the sovereignty of the self-existent God. Yet, both are descriptive of Jesus.

God introduces Himself as the self-existent God when He speaks to Moses: "This is what you are to say to the Israelites: 'I Am has sent me'" (Exodus 3:14). After that, the Jews considered "I Am" as a sacred name for God.

Jesus identified Himself with this name once in the temple while being questioned by the Jewish authorities. After a lengthy discussion, in which the Jews proudly claimed their relationship with Abraham, Jesus declared: "Before Abraham was, I Am" (John 8:58). They considered this remark blasphemous, so his enraged accusers picked up stones to kill Him. Jesus "hid Himself" from them and was not injured.

An unusual thing happened in the Garden when Jesus asked the soldiers whom they were seeking. They responded: "Jesus of Nazareth." When Jesus declared, "I am he," the soldiers all fell backward to the ground. An explanation is that the revelation of His identity as the self-existent God is more powerful than sinful man can withstand.

However, Jesus did not use His power to escape from His accusers as He did earlier, but He willfully submitted to them as a Lamb, knowing that they would lead Him to the Cross. We know the rest of the story: Though they crucified Him, He conquered death and ever lives as the Great I Am.

Prayer: Lord, help us remember Your greatness as the self-existent God, and appreciate Your submissiveness to the Cross for our sins. Amen.

[1] Mary, Did You Know? lyrics © Warner Chappell Music, Inc, Capitol Christian Music Group

Jesus said to them,
"I am
the *Bread of Life.*"

John 6:35

Christ, the Bread of Life

*C*hristian churches often have a service in which some form of bread and wine are taken ceremonially in remembrance of Christ's broken body. This service is rooted in Christ's teachings and Old Testament practice. Two of Christ's miracles involved these two elements: He turned water into wine in John 2 and multiplied the loaves of bread in John 6.

The Book of John records seven "I Am" statements of Christ. He not only identifies as the Great I Am, but also further defines the statement. We will discuss all these statements later. Two definitions refer to the ceremonial elements: "I am the Bread of Life," and "I am the Vine."

Throngs followed Jesus after the feeding of the 5,000. Even though He had gone to the other side of the Sea of Galilee, many still followed Him. Here He made the declaration, "I am the Bread of Life" which He repeated several times. Symbolically, He was comparing His coming to the provision of manna in the wilderness during the Hebrew exodus from Egypt. He would be food for the soul as manna was food for the body.

As we meditate upon this teaching, we see many comparisons. The Levitical sacrifices were called the "bread of God"; Jesus called Himself the "true bread from heaven." He calls Himself the "living bread," as opposed to manna that only lasted one day. The manna was just for the Hebrews; but as the Living Bread, Jesus "gives life to the world." The manna was available to all, but only those who gathered it were nourished by it. Jesus came to give life to the world, but only those who "receive" Him have power to become the sons of God.

Prayer: Lord, we thank You for coming as the Bread of Life. Help us to feed daily upon this Bread until we sit down with You in Your kingdom.

I am the
vine,
you are the
branches.

John 15:5

Christ, the Vine

*T*he Last Supper had ended. As they left the building, Jesus called the disciples' attention to the grapevines nearby, saying: "I am the true vine, and my Father is the vinedresser," (John 15:1), identifying His continued relationship with the Father. Then He added, "I am the vine, you are the branches" (v. 5), identifying His relationship with them.

The comparison of Christ to the vine is rich with symbolism: The vine grew from the root—as Christ came from the Father; the branches have no root so they draw strength from the vine. The branches bear fruit for the vinedresser; the disciples bear fruit for the glory of God.

A comparison can be made of the fruit of the vine to Christ's life. As the fruit is crushed to make wine, Christ was crushed for us. We remember His sacrifice as we take Communion.

Christ emphasizes the importance of the disciples' continued relationship with Him, "he who abides in Me and I in him, he bears much fruit," (v. 5). When they abide in Him they keep His commandments, are given the privilege of answered prayer, and bear fruit that glorifies the Father (vs.7,8).

Some people read this passage as a blank check for anything they desire, but we must remember the context: The promise of answered prayer is to those who abide in Christ, whose purpose is glorifying the Father by bearing fruit. Some prayer is not answered according to James 4:3: "You ask and do not receive, because you ask with wrong motives."

Three times Jesus mentions the importance of abiding in Him, to experience His love and a fullness of joy that is like no other. This love and joy is still available to all believers who daily abide in Him.

Prayer: Thank You for the privilege of studying Your Word, which teaches that we can have Your love and joy as we abide in You.

I am the *door;*
if anyone enters
through Me,
he will be saved.

John 10:9

Christ, the Door

*A*fter Jesus healed the blind man at Bethesda, some of the Jews rejected Him. Walking through the countryside, Jesus begins teaching His disciples, drawing examples from the nearby sheepfolds. He compares Himself both to the door or gate of the sheepfold, and the shepherds.

Observing shepherds leading flocks through the sheepfold door, Jesus said; "I am the door; if anyone enters through Me, he will be saved, and will go in and out and find pasture" (John 10:9, KJV). He was strongly declaring Himself as the one way to enter the kingdom of God.

The Jews who had denounced Him claimed the law as the only means of contacting God. Since their time, people have had other opinions—thinking that good works could gain entrance into the Kingdom. Others claim that many gods can lead to heaven.

But Jesus repeats that He is the only door. This truth was strongly preached by early believers: "Neither is there salvation in any other: for there is none other name under heaven given among men, whereby we must be saved" (Acts 4:12). Other Scriptures affirm this truth.

This teaching also clearly indicates that Jesus did not intend for His followers to live in isolation. The sheep did not spend all their time in the sheepfold but they "go in and out, and find pasture."

Christians experience life as other people do—sometimes in green pastures, sometime in the valley—but always with the security of the shepherd's presence by day and the serenity of the sheepfold at night with the shepherd sleeping at the door. As the Psalmist said: "In peace I will both lie down and sleep, For You alone, O LORD, make me to dwell in safety" (Psalm 4:8).

Prayer: Lord, we are thankful for Your death, the doorway to salvation, and Your resurrected life, where we safely abide daily.

I am the
good shepherd;
the good shepherd
lays down His life
for the sheep.

John 10:11

Christ, the Good Shepherd

As the small entourage walked through the countryside, Jesus continued teaching the disciples, this time drawing a comparison the disciples would have known from the Psalms: "I am the good shepherd; the good shepherd lays down His life for the sheep" (John 10:11).

The statement points to the primary essential of God's character—His goodness. Many actions might have been used as a confirmation of His goodness, but here Jesus chose to use His willingness to give His life for His sheep as indisputable evidence of His basic goodness. The disciples would not fully understand His meaning until after the Cross.

Sometimes when difficulties come, we tend to question why they happen. In those times, it is extremely important to remember this basic truth—God is essentially good. We can always trust His heart, even when we don't understand His actions. We may need some time to understand His purpose.

The second evidence of God's character Jesus gives in this passage in John 10 is that He is relational: "I am the good shepherd, and I know My own and My own know Me" (v. 14), The relationship was not limited to a few, but Jesus mentioned "other sheep" who would be brought into His fold. Thankfully, that reference includes you and me.

These two truths alone are enough to sustain us through the most difficult days of our lives. Sensing God's presence daily and trusting in His essential goodness, we can live the abundant life He promised (v.10).

Prayer: *Lord, when I don't understand what comes from Your hand, help me to trust Your heart—which is always good.*

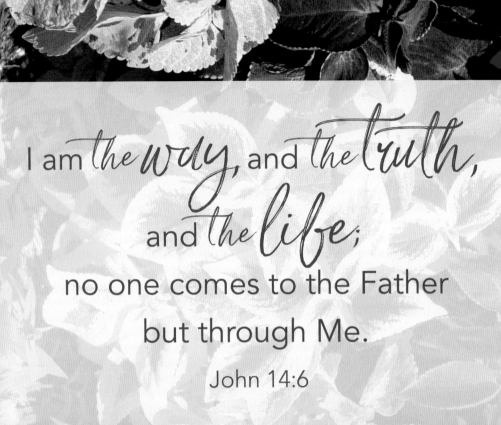

I am *the way*, and *the truth*, and *the life*; no one comes to the Father but through Me.

John 14:6

Christ, the Way, the Truth and the Life

After a relaxing dinner, conversation among friends sometimes can become very serious. Such was the case when Jesus and the disciples finished their Passover meal. Jesus initiated the conversation with a very surprising action; He arose from the table, laid aside His garments and began washing His disciples' feet.

After this action, the conversation continued in a serious vein, including personal interchange with both Judas and Peter. Judas then surprisingly left the room.

A quiet expectancy must have invaded the atmosphere of the room as Jesus continued talking. He had made the electrifying announcement that one of them would betray Him. He assured them of His love and emphasized the importance of love for each other. He then said He was going away and they would "know the way" where He was going.

In typical fashion, Thomas blurts out his doubts about knowing the way. Jesus' response is well known: "I am the way, and the truth, and the life; no one comes to the Father but through Me" (John 14:6).

Jesus not only declares that He is "the way" but affirms that He is the only way to the Father. His statement is true because He is "truth"—an attribute of God who cannot lie. The statement is not just a dogma to be believed but a manner of living, because He is the "life."

Some voices today try to tell us Jesus may be "a way" to heaven, but other ways exist as well. If that statement is true, then Jesus' statement that He is the way cannot be true because He would not be "truth" as He declared. We either have to believe He is "the only way" or not believe Him at all.

Prayer: Lord, we choose to believe that You are truth and the only way to the Father. Thank You for making that way known to us.

I am the resurrection and the life.

John 11:25

Christ, the Resurrection and the Life

So far, we have discussed characteristics of Jesus His listeners would have easily comprehended. They saw good shepherds, so they could easily view God that way. Other illustrations from their lives reinforced His teachings.

But the concept of Christ as Resurrection was different; resurrection was something in the unknown future. Jesus had raised two people from the dead—Jairus' daughter and the widow's son—but these were isolated incidents, not common occurrences.

So when Jesus delayed His coming to see Lazarus' until after his burial, his sisters Martha and Mary did not understand. They had no concept of Jesus as the Resurrection in their thinking.

Jesus used the occasion to illustrate the truth "I am the resurrection and the life" (John 11:25). To confirm this truth, He called Lazarus from the grave.

We know this resurrection was only an illustration because Lazarus later died a normal death. Through the centuries Christians have died at their appointed times; imagine the over-population problem if they did not.

But all those Christians died believing in Christ as the Resurrection. That belief is our greatest hope, the capstone of our theology. Paul discusses this hope in 1 Corinthians 15: "If we have hoped in Christ in this life only, we are of all men most to be pitied" (v. 19). But he confirms our hope of resurrection: "In a moment, in the twinkling of an eye, at the last trumpet; for the trumpet will sound, and the dead will be raised imperishable, and we will be changed" (v. 52).

Paul concludes the discussion with praise: "But thanks be to God, who gives us the victory through our Lord Jesus Christ" (v. 57). Our hope of victory over death is in Christ as the Resurrection.

Prayer: Lord, thank You for the hope we have because You are the Resurrection and the Life.

For no man can lay a foundation other than the one which is laid, which is *Jesus Christ.*

1 Corinthians 3:11

Christ, our Life's Foundation

*T*he stated purpose as we began this study was "to know God's Son, to understand His teaching and apply it to our lives." We have studied different pictures of Jesus from John's gospel. There is so much to know about Jesus that we understand why John said if it were all written, the world could not contain the books (John 21:25). We know following Jesus is a wise choice.

Jesus compared our choices to building a house "on a rock" or "on sand" (Matthew 7:24-27). The house on a rock would stand during a storm but the one on the sand would not. Our destiny is shaped by the choices we make.

How do we build our life with Jesus as our foundation? We make a decision—just as we would decide on a location to build a house. Choosing to build our life on Christ is an act of the will. We express that decision to Him in prayer.

The simplest prayer in the Bible was by one of the thieves on the cross beside Jesus. He prayed simply: "Jesus, remember me when You come into your kingdom" (Luke 23:42).

Another simple prayer was by a man who asked Jesus to pray for his child. When Jesus asked if he believed, his response was "I do believe; help my unbelief" (Mark 9:24). We need not have all the answers to our questions to start a relationship with Jesus.

John 3:16 has been called the theme of the Bible:

> For God so loved the world, that He gave His only begotten Son, that whoever believes in Him shall not perish, but have eternal life.

A simple prayer expressing our belief in Christ is the first step in building a life with Him. Expressing that prayer nails down the foundation of our life in Christ.

Prayer: Lord, we express our belief in You today. Help us let go of our unbelief. We want You as our life's foundation.

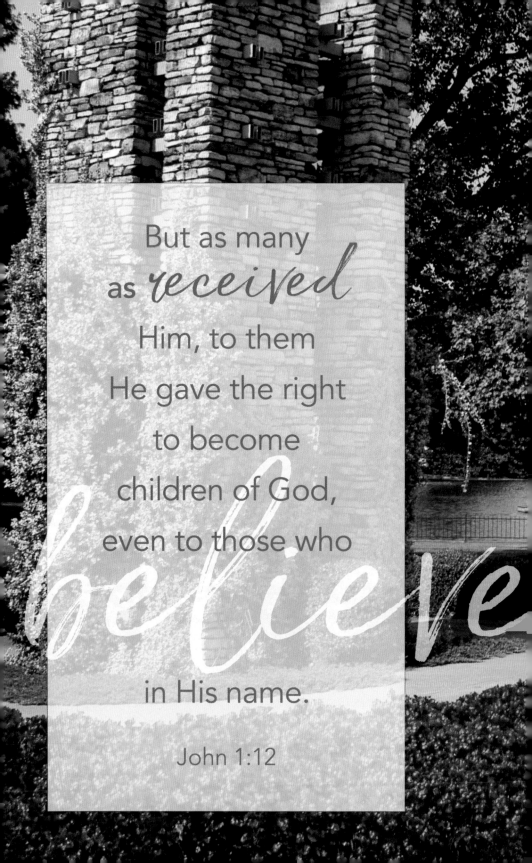

But as many as *received* Him, to them He gave the right to become children of God, even to those who *believe* in His name.

John 1:12

Receiving Christ

*B*elieving in Christ is more than having mental understanding that He lived; our belief becomes a foundational principle affecting our lives. The more we learn from the Scripture, the more we become aware of the change believing in Christ makes.

The Scriptures use many comparisons to explain what happens when we express our belief in Jesus. One comparison John uses is "receiving Christ" as a guest in our lives. In the opening chapter of his gospel, he tells that Jesus came to His own people, the Jews, but they did not "receive Him"—a phrase used of welcoming a guest. Then John writes in 1:12:

> But as many as received Him, to them He gave the right to become children of God, even to those who believe in His name.

He says that believing in Christ is like receiving Him as a guest in our lives. Keeping the thought of Jesus as a guest in our heart's home affects the way we live. And look whom we have become: "Children of God."

In the next verse John explains that believing in Christ is like being "born again"—not a natural birth but a spiritual birth:

> Who were born, not of blood nor of the will of the flesh nor of the will of man, but of God. (v. 13)

Jesus uses this same illustration with Nicodemus in John 3. This illustration enlarges on the thought that our belief brings us into the family as children of God; Jesus is not only a guest; He is our elder brother. Slowly the magnitude of our decision to follow Christ dawns on us, and we are just beginning to understand what has happened. Our belief in Jesus becomes a building block in the new life we find as His follower.

Prayer: Lord, we did not know all that happened when we believed in You. Thank You for accepting us in Your family and being a guest in our lives.

Therefore if anyone is in Christ, he is a *new* creature; the old things passed away; behold, new things have come.

2 Corinthians 5:17

Christ, Our Savior

*S*ome people think they have messed up too much to come to Christ. Saying this shows their lack of understanding of Jesus as Savior. Remember the Christmas story when the angels said this child to be born should be named Jesus "for He will save His people from their sins"? The salvation of sinners was the chief purpose of His coming.

The implication of this message is that all people have sins, something we know from other Scriptures. An old saying in the New England Primer was: "In Adam's fall, we sinned all."

The beauty of the salvation Jesus gives is that He offers forgiveness for all our sins: "In whom we have redemption, the forgiveness of sins" (Colossians 1:14). Forgiveness is for to all who believe in Him.

Something else happens when we believe. He not only forgives the sin we inherited from Adam, which caused us to make sinful choices, He gives us a new nature as a child of God:

> Therefore if anyone is in Christ, he is a new creature; the old things passed away; behold, new things have come. (2 Corinthians 5:17)

This new nature affects the way we think, but does not make us perfect human beings who never sin again. Learning the ways of the Lord is a process of growth. We are much like young children learning to walk and when we fall, we come again to ask for forgiveness. John makes this clear in his letter to early Christians: "My little children, I am writing these things to you so that you may not sin. And if anyone sins, we have an Advocate with the Father, Jesus Christ" (1 John 2:1).

Knowing our continual need of forgiveness may be why Jesus included the request for forgiveness in the Lord's Prayer.

Prayer: Lord, help us understand the totality of what You have done for us as Savior from our sins. We want to live in the new life You give us.

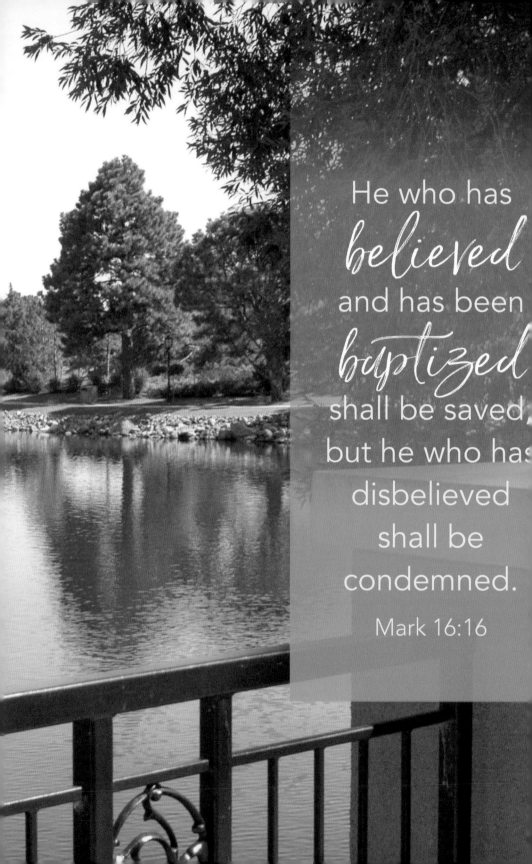

He who has *believed* and has been *baptized* shall be saved, but he who has disbelieved shall be condemned.

Mark 16:16

Water Baptism

*T*he Christian life is always lived in community; it is not merely a private way of thinking. From the Day of Pentecost, Christians were asked to make a public statement of their beliefs.

When onlookers on the Day of Pentecost asked Peter what they should do, He told them to repent and be baptized in the name of Jesus. Later about 3,000 people were baptized and became followers of Jesus. The Book of Acts records other accounts of water baptism as the church grew.

Jesus taught the importance of baptism; Mark records Him as saying:

> He who has believed and has been baptized shall be saved; but he who has disbelieved shall be condemned. (Mark 16:16)

Note that disbelieving results in condemnation; not failure to be baptized. The thief on the cross did not have opportunity to be baptized but Jesus told him he would be in paradise. Some people have physical reasons for not being baptized but their faith in Jesus will save them.

Baptism does not save us. It is the outward evidence of inward cleansing, a symbol of our identification with Christ's death and resurrection:

> And in Him you have been made complete . . . having been buried with Him in baptism, in which you were also raised up with Him through faith in the working of God, who raised Him from the dead. (Colossians 2:10,12)

Water baptism creates a reference point in our thinking to remind us of our identification with Christ as Savior. After our salvation, water baptism is another step in establishing our lives on the foundation of Jesus Christ.

Prayer: Lord, thank You for Your death and resurrection which brought us salvation. We identified with You when we were baptized for our faith.

For as often as you eat this bread
and drink the cup, you
proclaim the Lord's death
until He comes.

1 Corinthians 11:26

Communion

By the time Jesus came to earth, many Jewish traditions had been added to the law as originally given. The New Testament makes it clear that Christ is the fulfillment of the Law in the sight of God. New Testament believers are justified by God's grace through faith in Christ's death and resurrection and do not keep Jewish tradition.

From the beginning of the Church, most New Testament believers have practiced at least two rituals, or ordinances. These are Water Baptism and the Lord's Supper, also called Communion.

The Communion service is based on the Lord's teaching in the Gospels and Paul's writings. Jesus told the disciples to keep this practice His last night on earth:

> While they were eating, He took some bread, and after a blessing He broke it, and gave it to them, and said, "Take it; this is My body." And when He had taken a cup and given thanks, He gave it to them, and they all drank from it. And He said to them, "This is My blood of the covenant, which is poured out for many." (Mark 14:22-24)

Paul concludes his teaching by saying: "For as often as you eat this bread and drink the cup, you proclaim the Lord's death until He comes" (1 Corinthians 11:26).

Neither Water Baptism nor partaking in the Communion service saves us. Rather, they are acts of obedience to the Lord, giving us opportunity to identify with His death and resurrection and publicly declare our hope of His return. Both are to be done reverently and thoughtfully, in an attitude of appreciation for what Christ has done for us.

Regular participation in a Communion service is another foundational block in our new life in Christ. It becomes a lifelong practice for reaffirming our faith in the atoning work of Christ.

Prayer: Lord, we will be eternally grateful for what You did for us on the Cross. Help to remember it regularly with deep reverence.

Like *newborn babies*, long for the pure milk of the word, so that by it you may *grow*.

1 Peter 2:2

Building on God's Word

*A*fter we have taken the foundational steps of the Christian life, what does the rest of our life look like? The first believers in the New Testament had to settle this question, and so has every believer since then.

The Apostles were key figures in training early Christians. The Book of Acts tells us the believers "continued in the Apostle's doctrine." Their teaching is included in the New Testament, along with the writings of some others. God's Word is given to us to guide us as we grow in our faith in Jesus.

Jesus told Nicodemus that becoming a believer was like being born again. Peter enlarged on this thought in his epistle: "Like newborn babies, long for the pure milk of the word, so that by it you may grow" (1 Peter 2:2).

A key factor in our growth as a believer from infancy to maturity is our personal study of God's Word. The teachings we get at church expand our personal store of Bible knowledge.

The Bible is such a magnificent book that it appeals to both new readers and accomplished scholars who continue to plunge the depths of its meanings.

Our generation is blessed to have the Word of God accessible in many forms—print, digital, or audible. To establish the habit of daily reading, we need to have a regular time, a regular place and a definite plan for reading. Then, we discipline ourselves to follow that plan for reading and studying the Bible.

The beauty of Bible study is that we are not alone as we read. The Holy Spirit was given to be our guide as we read God's Word. John 16:13 says: "But when He, the Spirit of truth, comes, He will guide you into all the truth." As we read God's Word we become aware of the illumination of the Spirit to help our understanding.

Prayer: Lord, thank You for sending Your Spirit to help us understand Your Word. We want to grow in our knowledge of You.

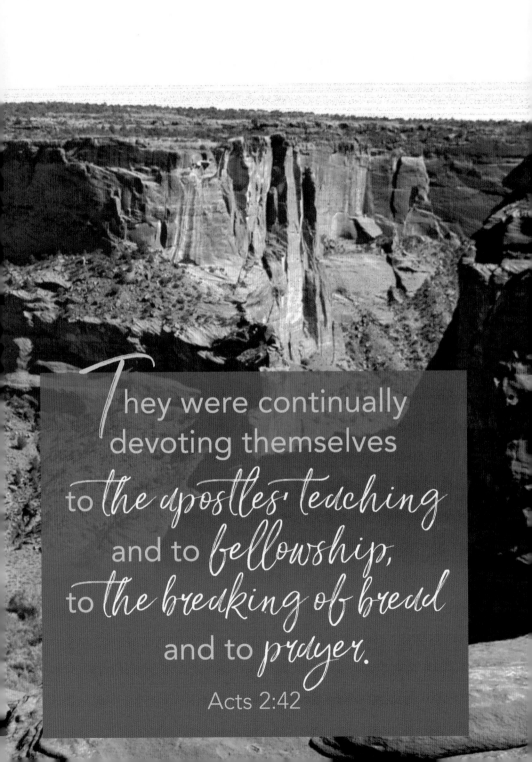

They were continually devoting themselves to the apostles' teaching and to fellowship, to the breaking of bread and to prayer.

Acts 2:42

Connecting to a Local Church

Jesus never intended for believers to live in isolation. When teaching the disciples to pray He used plural pronouns. This does not imply that we never pray for personal needs—we are also taught to "Be anxious for nothing, but in everything by prayer and supplication with thanksgiving let your requests be made known to God" (Philippians 4:6). But prayers should not be limited to personal needs only.

Some of Jesus' last words were: "Go into all the world and preach the gospel to all creation" (Mark 16:15). We call this command "The Great Commission." The people present on the Day of Pentecost shared their experience when they returned to their homes. After Pentecost, the disciples went separate ways and shared the good news of Jesus Christ to much of the then-known world.

It would be a physical impossibility for an individual Christian to fulfill this command of Jesus. Congregations of believers join with other congregations and systems are established to send missionaries around the world. By becoming involved with other believers in a local church, we too can participate in fulfilling the Great Commission.

Christians in an identifiable group can minister effectively to their community. Unbelievers receive teaching about Christ. Believers come together for prayer, worship and instruction in God's Word. The local church can give attention to specific needs within the body of believers, allowing Christian to show love one for another.

In writing about the early believers, Luke said, "They were continually devoting themselves to the apostles' teaching and to fellowship, to the breaking of bread and to prayer" (Acts 2:42). These four actions should be found in every church: *teaching, prayer, Communion*, and *fellowship*. Friendship with other believers is a strengthening building block in our Christian experience.

Prayer: Lord, thank You for our local church, a Christian community for our personal benefit and to help us fulfill the Great Commission.

Serve the Lord with gladness; Come before Him with *joyful singing*

Psalm 100:2

Becoming a Worshipper

*B*eing from Kansas, I understand the awe expressed in a quote from an old Indian chief, printed on the St. Louis Gateway arch: "I was born on the prairies where the winds blow free, with nothing to obscure the light of the sun."

The Psalmist David took this sense of awe of nature to adoration of God—from wonder to worship—in Psalm 8:1: "LORD, our Lord, how majestic is your name in all the earth! You have set your glory in the heavens" (NIV).

Something happens when a believer places trust in Christ. The Holy Spirit brings awareness of the presence of God, producing the spontaneous desire to worship. Believers come together to express this desire in Spirit-anointed worship services.

Old Testament worship included singing. Psalm 100:2 exhorts: "Serve the LORD with gladness; Come before Him with joyful singing." This exhortation challenges individuals to prepare for worship with anticipation.

When believers come together to worship, they are strengthened in their common faith. Coming together to worship is not an obligation to show what good Christians we are. Worship moves our minds from the problems of this life to the peace Jesus gives.

Corporate worship is for the glory of God and the edification of His people, not to exalt worship leaders or participants. Bringing children to church shares the faith with the next generation. Our worship should stir unbelievers to place their trust in God.

Maintaining our personal spirit of worship helps us face the difficulties of life. Paul and Silas demonstrated this with their feet in stocks in the Macedonian prison: "But about midnight Paul and Silas were praying and singing hymns of praise to God" (Acts 16:25). And we know the story. The ability to worship in times of difficulty indicates our growth in trust in God.

Prayer: Lord, help us maintain our sense of wonder that causes us to worship personally.

On the first day of every week each one of you is to *put aside and save,* as he may prosper.

1 Corinthians 16:2

Loving our Neighbors by Giving our Means

*J*esus summarized the Law as loving God and our neighbors. In writing to the Corinthians, Paul tells us what love looks like. I Corinthians 13:2 (AMP) says: "And if I have the gift of prophecy . . . and [possess] all knowledge; and . . . all [sufficient] faith . . . but do not have love [reaching out to others], I am nothing."

Paul says love is "reaching out to others" or becoming aware of their needs. This may be done in two ways—sharing who we are and what we have—another way of saying we share time and money.

The Old Testament was specific in ways Jews shared their money. The tithe of their increase was given at the temple, along with other special offerings.

The New Testament is not as specific. Jesus taught the principle of generosity with such statements as "Give, and it will be given to you" (Luke 6:38). He told about the widow's mite to show that how much we give is not as significant as how much we keep for ourselves.

The generous believers in Acts 2 shared everything they had. As churches grew and designated Sundays for meeting together, Paul encourages regular giving but does not mention an amount: "On the first day of every week each one of you is to put aside and save, as he may prosper . . ." (1 Corinthians 16:2). Giving was the means of supporting the church and its ministries.

Though the New Testament does not state specific amounts Christians should give, it seems logical that the first believers gave as the Old Testament trained them. Charitable giving is a means of showing our love for others, for God, and for His kingdom. Testimonies abound of God's blessing on those who faithfully give to Him. We'll talk later about giving our time.

Prayer: *Lord, You have been so generous with us; help us to be generous with Your Church and those in need.*

If I give all my possessions to feed the poor . . . *but do not have love,* it does me no good at all

1 Corinthians 13:3, AMP

Loving our Neighbors by Giving our Time

As important as it is for Christians to share material blessings with others, charitable giving is not always an indication of love. In Jesus' time coins were dropped into the temple coffers to make noise and impress others. Presumably the louder the noise, the greater the gift.

Jesus instructed His followers: "But when you give to the poor, do not let your left hand know what your right hand is doing" (Matthew 6:3.) In other words, do not make a show of your giving. Paul followed this teaching by saying: "If I give all my possessions to feed the poor . . . but do not have love, it does me no good at all" (1 Corinthians 13:3, AMP).

Sometimes people need someone to care more than they need financial assistance. The unfortunate man beside the road needed more than money; he needed the Good Samarian's merciful act of binding up his wounds.

Many people in our culture have been broken by life. Some suffer in silence; some are openly hurting. Compassionate Christians find many avenues of reaching out to minister to hurting neighbors. Sometimes it is a simple word of encouragement; other times it is ministering to obvious needs. But ministry does not happen until someone becomes aware of the need.

Reaching out to others requires sensitive eyes and ears to see needs, an innovative mind to know how to act, and a compassionate heart to motivate action. Needs may surface in unexpected places from unexpected people when we prepare our hearts to be ready to serve.

Sometimes, reaching out may require a temporary change in personal plans to meet the challenge of the present need. At other times, ministering to the needy may take a long-term commitment. Our willingness to be available as needed demonstrates a heart of genuine love.

Prayer: Lord, help me to become aware of the needs of others, to find ways to reach out—as if Your hand were ministering to their needs.

. . . like a wise master builder
I laid a foundation, and
another is building on it.
But each man must be careful
how he *builds* on it.

1 Corinthians 3:10

Commitment to Excellence

*O*ur purpose has been to know Jesus and understand His teaching. We reviewed basic steps of receiving Him into our lives. We observed the importance of personal Bible study with the Holy Spirit as our teacher.

We studied the value of water baptism and worshipping with other believers as a public witness. By uniting with a local church, we receive Bible teaching and share ministry to missions. We support the local church by giving time and money to its ministries.

Now we will study the teachings of Jesus and the apostles as guidelines for living the Christian life. Jesus indicates that there may be differences among Christian responses when He tells the parable of the sower. He likens His teaching to seed that falls on different kinds of ground, producing different results (Matthew 13:8). This teaching shows that believers may vary in their commitment to Christ.

Paul likened the Christian life to a building with Christ as the foundation:

> Like a wise master builder, I laid a foundation, and another is building on it. But each man must be careful how he builds on it. (1 Corinthians 3:10)

Later Paul compares building with "gold, silver and precious stones" or "wood, hay and stubble"—contrasting imperishable to perishable elements—or having either heavenly or earthly values. These teachings do not imply that it is OK to be just a "so-so" Christian who makes it to heaven, even though the life produces a weak harvest or builds a perishable building. The teachings challenge us to live now with eternity's values in view. We respond to the challenge for excellence with love for the Lord and a desire to give our best in return for all He gave for us.

Prayer: Lord, open our minds to Your teaching and our hearts to Your love. Show us how to be our best for You.

Getting Understanding 55

Blessed are the
poor in spirit,
for theirs is
the kingdom of heaven.

Matthew 5:3

Relationship with God— Humility

After telling us of Christ's early years and beginning ministry, Matthew presents the first teaching of Jesus as the "Sermon on the Mount." This may be a complete sermon, or a composite of several teachings.

"The Beatitudes" is the name scholars give to the opening teaching. In other places, Jesus has summarized the Law as loving God and others. The Beatitudes can be divided into those two categories—our relationship with God and with others. Jesus teaches about developing these relationships.

Matthew begins with "Blessed are the poor in spirit, for theirs is the Kingdom of Heaven" (Matthew 5:3). How strange these words may have sounded to Jesus' listeners. They frequently saw the prestigious display of some supposedly righteous persons. Now Jesus is saying that the humble person will possess the kingdom of heaven.

Jesus tells the story of two men who go up to pray. One, a Pharisee, tells God all the good things he has done. Beside him a publican, who will not even lift his eyes because of his sinfulness, humbly asks for mercy. Jesus shocked the listeners by saying the publican would be justified by God, not the Pharisee.

Jesus shows us that our attitude must be right when we approach God.

Humility is necessary in our first approach to God, and thereafter we strive to maintain a humble attitude before Him. James 4:10 tells us: "Humble yourselves in the presence of the Lord, and He will exalt you."

As we grow in our knowledge of God, we realize we are nothing without His goodness; that we owe everything to Him. When we thoroughly acknowledge this fact, humility is our natural response.

Prayer: *Lord, we acknowledge our unworthiness before You. We also know that because of Your grace, You receive us. For that grace we are humbly grateful.*

Blessed are *those who mourn,* for they shall be comforted.

Matthew 5:4

Relationship with God— Repentance

As Jesus continued teaching, His second statement was as surprising as the first: "Blessed are those who mourn, for they shall be comforted" (Matthew 5:3). This comparison sounds like a contradiction in terms. How can a person be blessed while mourning?

"Mourning" is the term used for the grief following the death of someone dear; "comfort" is brought by consoling friends. The possibility of being happy when mourning did not fit the definition of happiness then any better than it does now. People wondered what Jesus meant.

When we read these teachings as we are developing a relationship with God, the concept is easily understood. Pride keeps us from acknowledging our need of God or repenting of our sins. Jesus taught us to approach God in humility, recognizing that all we have is because of His grace.

Jesus' teaching on humility acknowledges that everyone since Adam has continued in sin. We recognize our own sinfulness and the tendency to defend ourselves even as Adam and Eve did—by passing the blame to someone else. We blame our failures on our human nature, or the way we were raised, or we say, "The devil made me do it." Human nature is reluctant to accept responsibility for sinful actions.

Jesus knew we would not know the joy of sins forgiven until we were genuinely sorrowful for our sinful condition, and approached God in repentance and "mourning" for our sins. Then, we could know the comfort that only He can give and understand our inheritance as a citizen of heaven.

How do we receive the comfort of God? Older translations of the Bible use the term "Comforter" for the Holy Spirit. The Holy Spirit brings the consolation of the Lord when we repent of our sins, assuring us of our salvation.

Prayer: Lord, thank You for welcoming us into Your presence when we repent of our sins. And thank You for the comfort of the Holy Spirit who brings joy to our hearts.

Blessed are
the meek:
for they shall
inherit the earth.

Matthew 5:5, KJV

Relationship with God— Submission

*J*esus continues teaching in the same format, with the unusual description of the blessed. "Blessed are the meek, for they shall inherit the earth" (Matthew 5:5). Many Psalms talk about those who will inherit the earth, but Psalm 37:11 specifically lists "the meek" as the earth's inheritors.

This statement would have been as puzzling to His listeners as the first two teachings were, even though this was a quote from Scripture. The Psalms had been around a long time and Israel had been in and out of captivity, sometimes a free nation but never ruling the earth.

This teaching is similar to the first one because it refers to the same attitude—an attitude of submission not self-assertiveness. Other translations use the words "gentle" or "humble." Jesus promised the "kingdom of heaven" to humble persons, now He says they will "inherit the earth." Without explanation, Jesus was trying to expand his listeners' thinking from present difficult circumstances to the future when His followers reign with Him (Revelation 20:6).

If we continue reading the teaching as progressively establishing our relationship with God, we see the continual need for humility and submission to God. We first come to Him in humility, aware of our complete dependency upon Him. He makes us a child of the kingdom of heaven. We mourn because of our sins until we receive the comfort of the Holy Spirit who puts joy in our hearts. We continue to submit to God in an attitude of meekness. He tells us of our future when we will reign with Him.

Three times Jesus said the person who walks this journey is "blessed." Those who have walked from sin to salvation, from hopelessness to joy, know that we are truly blessed with forgiveness for our past and hope for our future.

Prayer: Lord, how can we thank You for calling us to Yourself, from being nothing to inheriting a glorious future with You.

Blessed are *those who hunger and thirst* for righteousness, for they shall be satisfied.

Matthew 5:6

Relationship with God— Spiritual Hunger

Jesus continues telling His followers how to grow in faith after establishing relationship with God. He says, "Blessed are those who hunger and thirst for righteousness, for they shall be satisfied" (Matthew 5:6). Believers must continuously desire the things of God.

"Righteousness" was a hot topic to His listeners. They were familiar with Job's struggle with being righteous. Job pleaded his righteousness as something he put on "as a robe and a diadem" (Job 29:14), but he discovered that external righteousness was unacceptable to God.

Abraham was declared righteous by believing in the Lord (Genesis 15:6) but the Mosaic Law said righteousness came by keeping the Law: "It will be righteousness for us if we are careful to observe all this commandment before the LORD our God, jus as He commanded us" (Deuteronomy 6:25).

Jesus now declares that they may find righteousness when they desire it as much as they do food and drink. Later He said their righteousness had to exceed that of the Pharisees who carefully observed the Law (Matthew 5:20).

Jesus' teaching seemed puzzling, but His followers understood it better after His resurrection. The apostle Paul explains to the Romans:

> For what the law could not do, weak as it was through the flesh, God did: sending His own Son in the likens of sinful flesh and as an offering for sin, He condemned sin in the flesh, so that the requirement of the Law might be fulfilled in us, who do not walk according to the flesh but according to the Spirit. (Romans 8:3, 4)

Christians are in right standing before God because of faith in Jesus, not because of their own works. They have been set free from sin, but continue to walk in ways that honor God and fulfill His purpose in their lives (Romans 6:22).

Prayer: Lord, thank You that we gain right standing with You because of our faith in Jesus. Help us live in ways that show our gratitude.

Blessed are
the merciful,
for they shall receive mercy.

Matthew 5:7

Relationship to People— Showing Mercy

*T*he Sermon on the Mount gives instructions for loving God and loving others, the two principles Jesus used to summarize the Law. We studied the teaching on relating to God; we now look at ways to relate to people.

Jesus first teaching on relationship with people was: "Blessed are the merciful, for they shall receive mercy" (Matthew 5:7).

In a later teaching, He emphasized mercy by saying: "But go and learn what this means: 'I desire mercy, not sacrifice'" (Matthew 9:13 NIV). Other translations use the words "compassion" or "kindness" instead of mercy.

To understand what Jesus meant, we see that in Scripture those asking for mercy were social outcasts or persons in need. Blind beggars asked for mercy, as did the Canaanite woman requesting help for her daughter and a man requesting help for his son.

Jesus rebuked the scribes and Pharisees for enforcing the letter of the law and ignoring weightier matters such as mercy. In so doing, He called attention to their need for mercy. The awareness of our need for God's mercy motivates us to be merciful to others. All unbelievers are in need of God's mercy, not just persons in financial or physical need.

Note that Jesus implied that showing mercy did not replace the Pharisees' need to fulfill the Law: ". . . but these are the things you should have done without neglecting the others" (Matthew 23:23). Charitable deeds and acts of kindness can never replace our personal need to be right with God. God does not put all our actions on scales to see if our good deeds outweigh our bad ones. God looks for relationships—our relationship with Him comes first. That relationship—a relationship of love—influences all other relationships. We show mercy to others because we have received mercy from God.

Prayer: Lord, thank You for the mercy we received in forgiveness of sin; help us show Your mercy to others.

Blessed are
the pure in heart,
for they shall
shall see God.

Matthew 5:8

Relationship with Self— Guarding our Heart

*J*esus continues teaching on relationships by focusing on His listeners' spiritual condition. His previous teachings dealt with their relationship with God and other people. Now He challenges them to look inwardly at their own hearts:

> Blessed are the pure in heart, for they shall see God. (Matthew 5:8)

The Amplified Version uses this definition of pure in heart: "Those with integrity, moral courage, and godly character."

Something pure is simply what it is, without contamination or additives. When Jesus says a blessed person is one whose heart is pure, He refers to those whose hearts are uncontaminated by sin, those who maintain the pristine purity of being new creatures in Christ Jesus.

Solomon warned us: "Above all else, guard your heart, for everything you do flows from it" (Proverbs 4:23, NIV). Our desire is to do as Solomon said—to guard our heart, maintaining that purity of being cleansed from sins.

When we run cars through the car wash, they come out sparkling clean. We don't have to drive on muddy roads for that to change; cars soon become dingy with "road dirt" just from routine driving. Something similar happens in our hearts as we go through busy days. Our hearts can become contaminated with self-centered value systems of the world around us.

Just as we wash cars regularly to get rid of "road dirt," our regular return to God's Word helps us maintain purity of heart. Peter writes: "Now that you have purified yourselves by obeying the truth so that you have sincere love for each other, love one another deeply, from the heart" (1 Peter 1:22, NIV). As we absorb God's Word, our hearts are purified and filled with the love of God. We express that love in all our relationships.

Prayer: Lord, thank You for Your cleansing Word that purifies our hearts. Help us guard our hearts from the contamination of the world.

Blessed are *the peacemakers,* for they shall be called sons of God

Matthew 5:9

Peace in All Relationships

s Jesus continues to teach, He encourages His listeners to work for peace. "Blessed are the peacemakers, for they shall be called sons of God" (Matthew 5:9). In Romans, Paul encourages believers to work at peace. "So then we pursue the things which make for peace" (Romans 14:19). Here the Amplified Version says to "enthusiastically pursue peace."

Both of these Scriptures imply that peacemaking is a process not an event. We have to work at maintaining peace in relationships.

Paul encourage the Ephesians to maintain peace by overlooking some people's quirks: "Showing tolerance for one another in love, being diligent to preserve the unity of the Spirit in the bond of peace" (Ephesians 4:2,3). We tolerate our friends' quirks and they tolerate ours.

Paul emphasizes the power of prayer in maintaining peace: "In everything by prayer and supplication with thanksgiving let your requests be made known to God. And the peace of God . . . will guard your hearts and your minds" (Philippians 4:6,7).

Here Paul describes peace as the guardian of our hearts but in Colossians, he calls peace the ruler: "Let the peace of Christ rule in your hearts, to which indeed you were called in one body; and be thankful" (Colossians 3:15). The Amplified Version uses stronger language: "Let the peace of Christ be the controlling factor in your hearts [deciding and settling questions that arise]."

Some Christians, when faced with choices of action, base their decision on what brings peace. This verse in Colossians supports that practice.

Peace in relationships takes effort. Through prayer, we access the peace of God to guard our hearts, and to help us make decisions that give us peace

Prayer: Lord, You are the giver of peace; help us maintain our relationships in Your peace.

Blessed are those
who have been
persecuted
for the sake of
righteousness,
for theirs
is the kingdom
of heaven.

Matthew 5:10

Enduring Opposition

*H*ow blissful it would be if we had peace in all our relationships. Sadly, that is not a reality. Jesus knew it, so He gave instructions for our response to people who oppose us: "Blessed are those who have been persecuted for the sake of righteousness, for theirs is the Kingdom of Heaven" (Matthew 5:10). He then repeated the statement adding the instruction: "Rejoice and be glad, for your reward in heaven is great" (5:11).

We are to do everything we morally can to live in peace with others. When we have persecution, our first reaction is to be sure we have done nothing to cause it. Paul cautioned the believers: "If possible, so far as it depends on you, be at peace with all men" (Romans 12:18).

However, in spite of all we do, some people will oppose the gospel message with persecution. Christ forewarned of the possibility of persecution so the believers could be prepared with the appropriate response. If we are persecuted, we need to remember that no matter what people say or do to us, we are blessed by God and will be rewarded in heaven for our faith. This thought brings rejoicing to our hearts and helps us endure the persecution.

Paul instructed the Corinthians to respond positively to persecution by blessing rather than reviling the persecutor. Having this attitude would help them endure what came their way. "When we are reviled, we bless; when we are persecuted, we endure" (1 Corinthians 4:12).

As Jesus neared the end of His time on earth He warned His disciples about the possibility of persecution: "If they persecuted Me, they will also persecute you; if they kept My word, they will keep yours also" (John 15:20). Remembering that Jesus understands what we are going through helps us in times of persecution.

Prayer: Lord, if persecution comes our way, help us to endure by focusing on Your goodness and Your love.

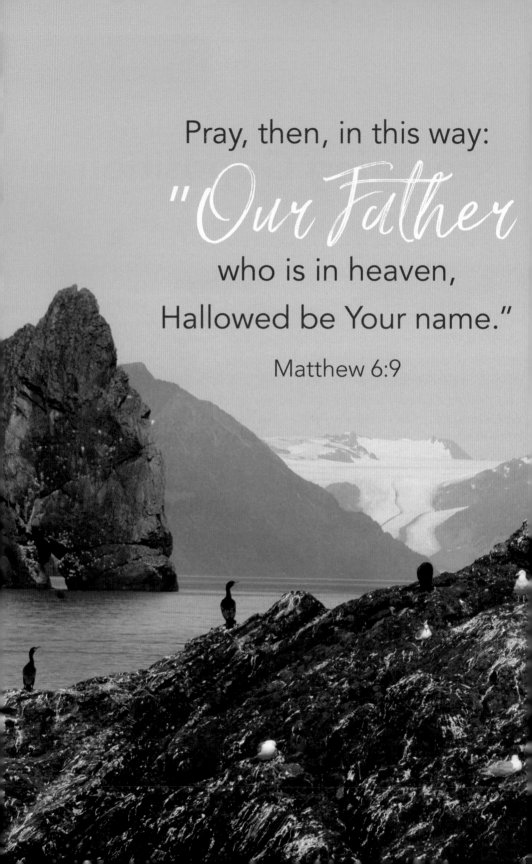

Pray, then, in this way:
"*Our Father*
who is in heaven,
Hallowed be Your name."

Matthew 6:9

Learning to Pray

*J*esus continues teaching by commenting on points of the Law and appropriate prayer. He warned against praying to be seen by others and challenged His listeners to pray with only God as audience. He said prayer is not to be ritualistic, and He gave a prayer we call "The Lord's Prayer."

Many of us learned this prayer in childhood and have heard it repeated on many occasions, as a prayer and a hymn. Jesus had just said that prayer should not be ritualistic, so we know He meant this prayer as a pattern when He said: "Pray in this way" (Matthew 6:9). As we study it we discover several elements—worship, intercession, petition, and praise.

We approach God in worship, remembering His identity and holiness: "Our Father who is in heaven, Hallowed be Your name." We acknowledge the greatness of His kingdom and intercede that earth will embrace heavenly values: "Your kingdom come. Your will be done, On earth as it is in heaven."

We move to petitioning for physical needs, referencing "daily bread" as a reminder of His provision of daily manna in the wilderness: "Give us this day our daily bread." We then petition for our spiritual need of forgiveness of sins, including our need to be forgiving people: "And forgive us our debts, as we also have forgiven our debtors."

Having physical and spiritual needs met, He adds a petition for guidance into right paths, away from the temptations around us: "And do not lead us into temptation, but deliver us from evil."

The prayer closes with a prayer of praise, acknowledging God's supremacy: "For Yours is the kingdom and the power and the glory forever. Amen" (Matthew 6:9-13).

With this pattern for prayer, we know we can come to the Father regularly in worship to express our personal needs and intercede for others, always humbly maintaining our need of forgiveness and acknowledging His supremacy.

Prayer: Lord, how grateful we are for the privilege of prayer, and the assurance that You hear and respond.

Eagerly pursue and seek to acquire this *love,* make it your aim, your great quest. . . .

1 Corinthians 14:1, CAV

Love

*P*aul's writings help us as we continue our quest of learning to build our lives with Christ as the foundation. Jesus defined the Christian life as loving God, and our neighbors as ourselves. Paul enlarges on that definition:

> But the fruit of the Spirit is love, joy, peace, patience, kindness, goodness, faithfulness, gentleness, self-control. (Galatians 5:22, 23)

Paul describes the result of the Holy Spirit in the life of a believer, comparing this result to fruit on a vine:

> I am the vine, you are the branches; he who abides in Me and I in him, he bears much fruit, for apart from Me you can do nothing. (John 15:5)

The manifestation of the fruit of the Spirit should be a natural outgrowth of our relationship with Christ, the Vine.

As we analyze the list Paul gives, we observe that describes love in our relationship with God, with others and ourselves, the same areas Jesus said we should show love. Our relationship with God is one of "love, joy, and peace." Our love for others is evidenced by our "patience, kindness and goodness." We show love for ourselves—or self-respect—with "faithfulness, gentleness and self-control."

Paul warns the Corinthians that even spiritual manifestations and charitable actions could be performed without true love for God. His description of genuine love is very similar to the description he gives to the Galatians. This love, he says, "never fails" and is the greatest of gifts.

Paul follows with the admonition to "Pursue love" (1 Corinthians 14:1). The Classic Amplified Version translates this verse: "Make love your aim, your great quest." The quest for love in all relationships is a goal worth giving our lives to.

Prayer: Lord, we are grateful for Your love for us; help us to show that love to others.

... for the

joy

of the Lord

is your

strength,

Nehemiah 8:10

Joy

Joy, when mentioned in the Bible, often refers to the emotion that follows a victory in battle.

When David and Saul returned from battle, the women met them with "joy and with musical instruments" (1 Samuel 18:6). When Solomon was anointed king, there was so much rejoicing that the earth shook (1 Kings 1:40).

Much later, when the people returned from captivity, they began weeping; Ezra and Nehemiah reminded them that they should not weep but rejoice for what God had done "Do not be grieved, for the joy of the Lord is your strength" (Nehemiah 8:10). In all of these occasions, people experienced joy as they thanked God for victory.

When the angels announced Jesus' birth, they said they had news of "great joy" because a Savior had been born. His coming would save His people from their sin. The victory over sin is our constant source of joy.

Paul writes to the Galatian Church that joy is fruit of the Spirit's working in their lives: "But the fruit of the Spirit is love, joy, peace, patience, kindness, goodness, faithfulness, gentleness, self-control" (5:22, 23).

From our knowledge of joy in the Bible, we know Paul is not talking about happiness—the emotion that is because of good "happenings"—but joy is something much deeper. The joy that is the fruit of the Spirit is because Jesus has given us victory over sin.

Unpleasant circumstances can steal our happiness, but they should never steal our joy. Paul talks about joy in writing to the Philippians, and challenges them to "Rejoice in the Lord always; again I will say, rejoice!" (4:4). He continues by telling them rejoicing is possible as they remember the Lord is near, and they may express their needs to Him in prayer (4:6).

Prayer: Lord, help us to maintain the joy of forgiven sin and our relationship with You. May we never let what happens to us steal that joy.

And the *peace* of *God* that surpasses all understanding will *guard your hearts and minds* in Christ Jesus.

Philippians 4:7, NET

Peace

The word peace was used by early believers both as a greeting and when bidding farewell, as common as our "hello" and "goodbye." When Paul includes peace as a fruit of the Spirit, he is talking about something much deeper than a greeting. He is talking about the peace that "surpasses all understanding" (Philippians 4:7, NET).

How does peace go beyond our understanding? God is the source of this peace that is more than the absence of conflict, our usual definition of peace. One of Jesus' names is "Prince of Peace." He came so that people could have peace with God. The peace we have comes from our relationship with Him, not from what is going on around us.

Paul challenges the Philippians to let this peace "guard" their hearts. The implication is that peace is the keeper of their hearts, much like the police who patrol our streets. He challenges the believers to center their minds on things that are true, honest, and of good report (v 8). Too often, our troubled minds rob us of the peace of God. When making a decision, a good question to ask ourselves is "What gives us peace?"

Paul underscores this teaching by saying: "And what you learned and received and heard and saw in me, do these things. And the God of peace will be with you" (v 9, NET). The emphasis here is on the word *do*. When we act on the teachings of God's Word, we know the God of peace is with us.

We experienced the peace of God at salvation. We can live His peace when we control our thought life, reminding ourselves of God's great provision for us. His presence is with us, giving us peace in the most difficult circumstances.

Prayer: Thank You for the peace of God that does go beyond our natural understanding. In spite of what is going on around us, You are always there, giving us peace.

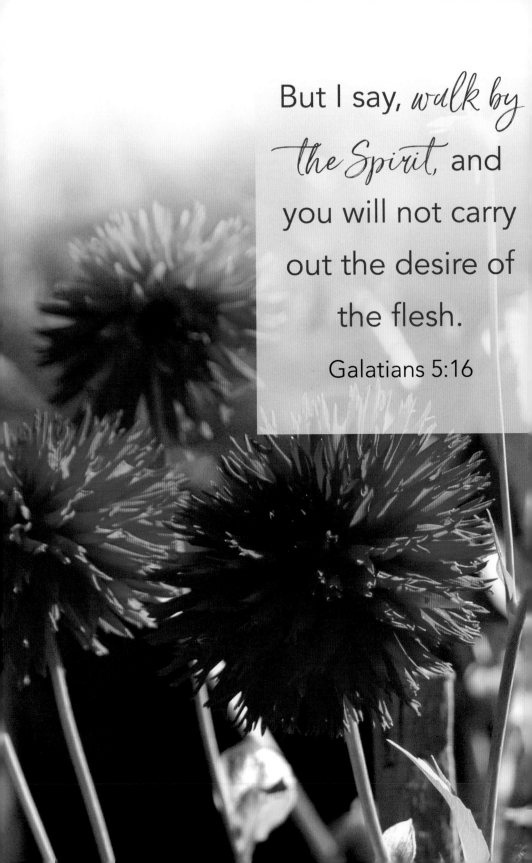

But I say, *walk by the Spirit*, and you will not carry out the desire of the flesh.

Galatians 5:16

Sins of the Flesh

*B*efore Paul lists the fruit of the Spirit, he challenges believers to "walk by the Spirit, and you will not carry out the desire of the flesh" (Galatians 5:16). He refers to the conflict they experience when natural desires war against the teachings of the Spirit.

Paul also lists the deeds of the flesh that conflict with the fruit of the Spirit. As we examine this list, we see the areas of conflict are relationship with God, with others, and with our self-control. Our relationship with God can be affected by practices such as idolatry, sorcery, and heresies.

From the Old Testament we know idolatry was Israel's downfall. But before we become too judgmental, we should ask ourselves, "Is anything I have, or anything I do, becoming more important to me that my relationship with God?" If so, we may be as guilty of idolatry as Israel was.

True believers are not likely to become involved with sorcery, which some translations list as "witchcraft" or "drug-induced" spiritual experiences. But these practices are rampant in today's culture. The Spirit of God helps us to be victorious over these practices if we encounter them.

Heresy may be our greatest challenge. Our teaching must be rooted in the Word of God to encounter subtle falsehoods around us. We hear things like "it doesn't matter what you believe, just so you are sincere." But if you believe anything contrary to God's Word, you can be "sincerely wrong."

Paul concludes the passage as he started it; he challenges believers to live their beliefs.

"If we live by the Spirit, let us also walk by the Spirit." (Galatians 5:25)

A teacher once summarized this verse for a class I was in: "If you talk the talk, be sure you walk the walk!"

Prayer: Lord, help us make the right decisions when we experience the conflict of our natural desires and the working of the Spirit.

. . . walk in a manner worthy of the Lord . . . strengthened with all power . . . for the attaining of all steadfastness and

patience.

Colossians 1:11

Patience

As we continue studying the fruit of the Spirit, we observe that Paul moves from our relationship to God to our relationship with people. The first word Paul uses for this human relationship is "patience," or "long-suffering."

Patience is the ability to tolerate difficult situations without getting upset. Most relationships among people—whether family or friends—will at times encounter "difficult situations." When caught in such a situation, we have various possibilities of response.

The immediate response often is impatience, showing our disapproval of the action. Impatience can lead to outbursts of anger or other actions that usually complicate the situation. Paul clearly declares these reactions are manifestations of the natural man.

Showing tolerance of a situation does not mean you approve the action. It only shows your willingness to take time to work out a solution for the problem. In these times believers have the help of the Holy Spirit who, according to Colossians 1:11, strengthens us "with all power, according to His glorious might, for the attaining of all steadfastness and patience." Patience with others in difficult situations reveals the fruit of the Spirit in our lives.

Peter warns believers that there may be times when they do what is right, but will not be appreciated. This kind of circumstance also calls for a patient response:

> For what credit is there if, when you sin and are harshly treated, you endure it with patience? But if when you do what is right and suffer for it you patiently endure it, this finds favor with God. (1 Peter 2:20)

It helps to know when we are unappreciated by others, that God sees and looks upon us with favor if we are patient in the situation.

Prayer: Lord, forgive us for those times we have been intolerant and thank You, for the times You have helped us endure difficult situations with patience.

Be kind

to one
another,
tender-
hearted,
forgiving
each
other, just
as God
in Christ
also has
forgiven
you.

Ephesians 4:32

Kindness

*P*aul lists the action of kindness after the reaction of patience as the fruit of the Spirit seen in our relationship with others. The Spirit not only affects how we respond to others but how we treat them.

The word we are looking at is most often translated "kindness," but occasionally translated "gentleness," which suggests handling something fragile. The picture that comes to my mind is of a housewife handling expensive crystal stemware. She is very cautious because she not only appreciates its beauty but also is aware of its fragility. We should keep these two factors in mind in our relationships with other people.

The people we contact daily are highly valued in the eyes of God, and their human spirit is fragile and easily damaged. A harsh word may correct other people's actions but injure their spirit. The Holy Spirit can help us deal kindly in our relationships, giving consideration for the needs and feelings of others.

It is easy to show kindness to people who think and act like we do. Our compassion for the needy causes us to treat them with kindness and consideration. However, when we encounter people with different opinions and inappropriate actions we sometimes have problems. Disrespect for the opinions of others is rampant in our culture, and we can fall easily into that pattern of behavior.

With kindness, we can respect another's opinion without agreeing with them. We can disapprove of another's actions and still treat them kindly. Paul's writing to the Ephesians indicates that forgiveness may be the key to kindness:

> Be kind to one another, tenderhearted, forgiving each other, just as God in Christ also has forgiven you. (Ephesians 4:32)

We can be forgiving to the errant by remembering our forgiveness from God.

Prayer: Lord, help us in all our relationships to be as kind to others as You have been kind to us.

. . . you yourselves are full of *goodness,* filled with all knowledge and able also to admonish one another.

Romans 15:14

Goodness

Goodness is the next character trait Paul lists as a fruit of the Spirit. Almost all English translations of the Scripture use the same word. Only a few use the word "generosity." It seems we all know what goodness is; we just have difficulty finding another word to explain it.

In the Old Testament, goodness refers primarily to the character of God. Many psalms praise God for His goodness. A typical expression is: "How great is Your goodness, Which You have stored up for those who fear You" (Psalm 31:19).

However, in the New Testament, goodness is found only in Paul's writings, and always as a character trait of the believers:

> And I myself also am persuaded of you, my brethren, that ye also are full of goodness, filled with all knowledge, able also to admonish one another. (Romans 15:14, NASB)

Paul seems to say that the Spirit produces essential goodness in the life of the believer, which is revealed in relationships with others.

Our minds easily go back to the creation story when God pronounced each phase of creation "good." Trees were different from birds and mountains but they all were "good" as each existed to fulfill His purpose for them. It is easy to see that as "new creations" in Christ, believers also are essentially "good" as they fulfill the purpose for which they were created.

Believers have the responsibility is to discover the gifts and talents God has placed within them. Then, we spend our lives fulfilling His purpose for us. We do not do this alone, but with the help of His Spirit.

A familiar psalm states: "Surely His "goodness . . . will follow me all the days of my life" (Psalm 23:6). Any goodness we have flows from His goodness within us.

Prayer: *Lord, how grateful we are that You are a good God, and You share that goodness with us by Your Spirit.*

...walk by the *Spirit,* and you will not carry out the desire of the flesh.

Galatians 5:16

Sins of the Flesh
in Relationships with People

*W*hen considering the fruit of the Spirit in relationships with others, it is important to contrast them with the actions of the natural man. Paul wants us to know the difference. In Galatians 5:19-21, he states:

> Now the deeds of the flesh are evident, which are: immorality, impurity, sensuality . . . enmities, strife, jealousy, outbursts of anger, disputes, dissensions, factions, envying. (Galatians 5:19-21)

We can categorize these actions as inappropriate physical, mental, and emotional behaviors. Jesus' teaching on maintaining purity of thought illustrates these layers of concern in this area: "But I say to you that everyone who looks at a woman with lust for her has already committed adultery with her in his heart" (Matthew 5:28).

Paul uses several nouns to describe conflicts between people. Two words get to the root of many conflicts in relationships: jealousy and envy. We can respond to this list in different ways: We can justify our failures, saying we are only human and continue behaving in natural ways, or, we can condemn ourselves with every failure.

Paul gives another possible response: "Now those who belong to Christ Jesus have crucified the flesh with its passions and desires" (Galatians 5:24). We don't literally nail ourselves to a cross, but with the help of the Holy Spirit we reject natural tendencies and willfully choose to follow the Spirit's enablement. "If we live by the Spirit, let us also walk by the Spirit" (5:25).

And what if we fail? Paul says: "Brethren, even if anyone is caught in any trespass, you who are spiritual, restore such a one in a spirit of gentleness; each one looking to yourself, so that you too will not be tempted" (Galatians 6:1). We forgive others for failures, knowing we need forgiveness at times. We "bear one another's burdens, and thereby fulfill the law of Christ" (6:2).

Prayer: Lord, our desire is to please You in all ways, including our relationships with others. Help us to be sensitive to Your Spirit so we respond appropriately in difficult situations.

But the fruit of the Spirit is . . .
faithfulness, gentleness, self-control.

Galatians 5:22

Faithfulness and Gentleness

The last three qualities listed as fruit of the Spirit apply to how we take care of ourselves. Jesus summarized the Law in two sentences—loving God with all our hearts and loving our neighbor as ourselves. Too often we read this as a two-part command, ignoring the implied third one—that we should love ourselves. Loving ourselves means that we are as patient and kind to ourselves as we are to our neighbor.

Faithfulness and gentleness are the first two character traits mentioned in this group. Faithfulness, like other traits that reflect the character of God, is a bit difficult to define. Most translators do not use any other word. One version uses the word "fidelity" which ironically the dictionary defines as "faithfulness."

In describing God's faithfulness, Lamentations 3:22-23 says:

> The LORD'S loving kindnesses indeed never cease, For His compassions never fail. They are new every morning; Great is Your faithfulness.

God's faithfulness is recognized because of His consistency of character. He is the same one day as the next. That principle of consistency should be foundational in the life of the believer.

"Gentleness" is a term very similar to the word for "kindness," the trait we observed earlier as important in our relationship with others. However, we need to extend that same kindness and gentle treatment to ourselves.

Too often, we drive ourselves to achieve goals or we blame ourselves for failures. Sometimes in our busy lives, we ignore our physical needs to the detriment of our health. Taking care of ourselves is not a matter of pride nor is neglecting ourselves an indication of humility. Taking care of ourselves shows an understanding of Jesus' teaching that we are to respect ourselves. We treat ourselves with the kindness and gentleness we show to others.

Prayer: Lord, help us to follow Your example of faithfulness. Forgive us if we misunderstand Your teaching, and help us also to extend kindness to ourselves.

... able to marshal and direct our energies *wisely*

Galatians 5:22-25, MSG

Self-control

*P*aul adds self-control to conclude the list of traits that are fruit of the Spirit in the life of the believer. What a challenging thought—that a person who is self -disciplined in all areas of life is manifesting the fruit of the Spirit.

Paul is not suggesting listing rules and keeping them; that would be reverting to the legalism of the Law. Instead, he recommends that the inward control of the Spirit enables the believer to make good decisions in all areas of life—physical, mental and spiritual.

The Message sums up the list of the fruit of the Spirit with this paraphrase:

> But what happens when we live God's way? He brings gifts into our lives, much the same way that fruit appears in an orchard—things like affection for others, exuberance about life, serenity. We develop a willingness to stick with things, a sense of compassion in the heart, and a conviction that a basic holiness permeates things and people. We find ourselves involved in loyal commitments, not needing to force our way in life, able to marshal and direct our energies wisely.

> Legalism is helpless in bringing this about; it only gets in the way. Among those who belong to Christ, everything connected with getting our own way and mindlessly responding to what everyone else calls necessities is killed off for good—crucified. (Galatians 5:23,24, MSG)

Instead of seeking our own way or simply following the crowd, the self-disciplined person learns to follow the leading of the Spirit: "Able to marshal and direct our energies wisely." The Spirit produces the appropriate fruit in all relationships—our walk with God, our interaction with others, and our personal life. When we falter, the Spirit is there to help us be the person God intended us to be.

Prayer: Lord, we want to be that person—one who allows the Spirit to produce fruit in all our relationships. Help us to live so that is a possibility.

But I say,
walk by the $\mathcal{Spirit}$,
and you will not carry out
the desire of the flesh.

Galatians 5:16

Sins of the Flesh
as Wrong Expressions of a Self-life

*P*aul completes his list of deeds of the flesh with behaviors revealing an absence of self-control:

> Now the deeds of the flesh are evident . . . drunkenness, carousing, and things like these, of which I forewarn you, just as I have forewarned you, that those who practice such things will not inherit the kingdom of God. (Galatians 5:19, 21)

The list is a second warning, as he wants them to take it seriously. It is open-ended, suggesting that believers use good judgment about behaviors not included, such as recreational drug-abuse prevalent in our culture. He does include "carousing" which some translations list as "wild parties."

When we read this exhortation, our mind goes readily to other letters on the subject. Ephesians 5:18 clearly warns against drunkenness: "And do not get drunk with wine, for that is dissipation, but be filled with the Spirit." However in 1 Timothy 5:23 he writes: "No longer drink water exclusively, but use a little wine for the sake of your stomach and your frequent ailments."

In cultures where social drinking is widely acceptable, some believers see the letter to Timothy as approval of the use of alcoholic beverages. However, the text clearly indicates Paul is approving medicinal use and not social drinking.

No one ever intends to become an alcoholic, but addictions begin with the first drink. Avoiding that "first drink" is the best way to avoid drunkenness and addiction.

Personally, I have seen so many lives broken by the use of alcohol that I choose to avoid it completely, not only for myself but also as an example to others. Instead, I choose to live life as Paul said, with the indwelling presence of the Holy Spirit who fills me with the joy of the Lord. That is the life I want to share with all my friends and family.

Prayer: Lord, thank You for Your Holy Spirit who fills us with greater joy than anything this world offers.

. . .you also, as *living stones* are being built up as a spiritual house for a holy priesthood . . .

1 Peter 2:5

Living Stones

*T*he colorful apostle Peter is one many people relate to because he was so candid. Thankfully, Jesus looked beyond his weaknesses and saw what he could become, calling him a "rock," a small stone. Later, when Peter makes his bold recognition of Christ's true identity, Jesus makes an interesting play on words: "I also say to you that you are Peter, and upon this rock I will build My church" (Matthew 16:18), comparing Peter as a small stone to Himself, the larger rock on which the Church would be built.

In his writings, Peter uses the same figure in describing the Church:

> And coming to Him as to a living stone which has been rejected by men, but is choice and precious in the sight of God, you also, as living stones, are being built up as a spiritual house . . . (1 Peter 2:4,5)

Peter very appropriately describes Christ as a "living" stone as He is "Life" (John 1). All followers have life in Christ and are also living stones, joined together as a holy priesthood.

Three Gospel writers refer to Christ as the one rejected by builders who became the cornerstone. Paul uses this same comparison:

> Having been built on the foundation of the apostles and prophets, Christ Jesus Himself being the corner stone, in whom the whole building, being fitted together, is growing into a holy temple. (Ephesians 2:20, 21)

In His teachings, Jesus used the comparison of building our individual lives on the rock; He is that foundation, and we carefully build according to His teaching. The expansion of this teaching shows that Christian life is to be lived in community, which we call "the Church." When we connect with other believers in a church, we become the temple of the Lord.

Prayer: Lord, thank You for leading me to the Rock as a foundation for my life; and thank You for the Christian community, the temple of the Lord.

. . . Christ also *suffered for you,* leaving you an example for you to follow in His steps.

1 Peter 2:21

Accepting Suffering

*O*ne of the most difficult questions asked of Christians is this: "Why do believers suffer illness and even harder things, like persecution?" Some try to tell us that suffering is either because of sin in our life or lack of faith. These issues might be causes at times but they certainly are not the only reasons Christians suffer.

Two of Paul's closest helpers dealt with physical problems. If they had been ill because of sin or lack of faith, Paul would have dealt with them. Instead, he left Trophimus at Miletus to recover from his illness (2 Timothy 4:20). He told Timothy to treat his frequent ailments (1 Timothy 5:23). Sometimes the physical body breaks down, and we follow this example of treating it as necessary.

Both Paul and Peter deal with other difficulties Christians face, particularly forms of persecution because of their faith. We think of persecution as being in the past but Christians are suffering today for their faith in many places.

Peter reminds us that Christ left us the example of suffering:

> For you have been called for this purpose, since Christ also suffered for you, leaving you an example for you to follow in His steps. (1 Peter 2:21)

Peter encourages believers to maintain a good attitude when persecuted, not defensive but gentle and reverent. He tells them to maintain a good conscience before God, and to be ready to explain their faith.

Paul reminded believers that God's love is still with us, even in persecution:

> For I am convinced that neither death, nor life, nor angels, nor principalities, nor things present, nor things to come, nor powers, nor height, nor depth, nor any other created thing, will be able to separate us from the love of God, which is in Christ Jesus our Lord. (Romans 8:38, 39)

Prayer: Lord, help us be more aware of Your love than we are of any difficulty we are enduring.

Blessed is he who reads and those who hear the words of the prophecy.

Revelation 1:3

Beatitudes of Revelation

*E*arlier, we studied the Beatitudes of Matthew, those familiar passages that begin with the word "blessed." Less familiar are seven similar passages in Revelation beginning with the same word. In both passages, *blessed* means more that being happy; it includes having favorable circumstances.

The Book of Revelation opens with a declarative statement of blessing to those who read it: "Blessed is he who reads and those who hear the words of the prophecy, and heed the things which are written in it" (1:3).

This statement encourages reading the prophecy for its message of hope. When reading Revelation, we have to resist the tendency to bog down in the highly symbolic details. In the end, we get a vivid description of our eternal home.

The next blessing listed in Revelation also offers hope: "And I heard a voice from heaven, saying, 'Write, "Blessed are the dead who die in the Lord from now on!" 'Yes,' says the Spirit, 'so that they may rest from their labors, for their deeds follow with them'" (14:13).

This reference comes at difficult time on earth when believers in Christ are being martyred. It refers to a particular group but reaffirms the "blessed hope" of all believers:

> For the grace of God has appeared, bringing salvation to all men, instructing us to deny ungodliness and worldly desires and to live sensibly, righteously and godly in the present age, looking for the blessed hope and the appearing of the glory of our great God and Savior, Christ Jesus. (Titus 2:11-13)

No matter what comes to us in this life, we have the hope of being forever with the Lord.

Prayer: Lord, thank You for the blessed hope we have for a future with You, help us to honor You with the way we live now.

... for the *Son of Man is* **coming** at an hour when you do not think He will.

Matthew 24:44

Watchfulness

*I*n his vision, John hears a "loud voice" instructing angels to "pour out seven bowls of the wrath of God." This is figurative language of God's judgment coming on all creation. Parenthetically, before the final wrath is outpoured, the angel inserts a blessing to Christ's followers:

> Behold, I am coming like a thief. Blessed is the one who stays awake and keeps his clothes, so that he will not walk about naked and men will not see his shame. (Revelation 16:15)

This reminder of Christ's coming repeats a warning given to the church at Sardis earlier:

> So remember what you have received and heard; and keep it, and repent. Therefore, if you do not wake up, I will come like a thief, and you will not know at what hour I will come to you. (3:3)

Paul had made a similar comparison in his letter to the Thessalonians. Jesus taught the importance of being ready for His return with His parable of the virgins—five were prepared and five were not. He also made the comparison of His coming as a thief in the night.

> For this reason you also must be ready; for the Son of Man is coming at an hour when you do not think He will. (Matthew 24:44)

These teachings challenge us to prepared for Christ's coming with confidence and not fear. First, we watch the time in which we live to see what God is doing. Then, when we see prophecy being fulfilled, we are to "straighten up and lift up your heads, because your redemption is drawing near" (Luke 21:28). Luke's instruction to "straighten up" is our challenge to watch our hearts to be sure we are ready to meet Him.

Prayer: Lord, as the old hymn says, "With joy we welcome Your returning" because we have trusted our lives in Your hands.

Blessed are those who are invited to the *marriage supper of the Lamb.*

Revelation 19:9

Future Joy

*T*he next blessing mentioned in Revelation refers to a time of joy in heaven:

> Then he said to me, "Write, 'Blessed are those who are invited to the marriage supper of the Lamb.'" (Revelation 19:9)

Not much is known about this event, as it is not mentioned elsewhere in Scripture. However, the previous verses make it clear that the wedding is figurative language of the union of believers and Christ.

> Let us rejoice and be glad and give the glory to Him, for the marriage of the Lamb has come and His bride has made herself ready." It was given to her to clothe herself in fine linen, bright and clean; for the fine linen is the righteous acts of the saints. (19:7,8)

The Gospels make many references to weddings. The first miracle was at a wedding (John 2). Later, Jesus told a parable teaching the importance of being appropriately dressed for a wedding (Matthew 22), and another parable about waiting for the bridegroom (Matthew 25).

Matthew reports Jesus comparing His disciples to friends of the bridegroom who did not fast.

> The days will come when the bridegroom is taken away from them, and then they will fast. (9:15)

Mark and Luke include this same statement in their writings.

John the Baptist compared himself to the friend of the bridegroom when people first became aware of Jesus' ministry (John 3:29). Though there is much that we don't know about this event, there is something we do know. The union of Christ and His followers is a time of great rejoicing for those who have made themselves ready.

Prayer: *Lord, thank You that You have clothed us in Your righteousness so we can be ready to meet You on this joyous day.*

Blessed and holy
is the one who has a part in
the first resurrection;
over these the second death
has no power.

Revelation 20:6

Preparedness

*L*ife after death was a matter of controversy at the time Jesus lived on the earth. The Pharisees believed that there was life after death; the Sadducees did not. On several occasions, the Sadducees challenged Jesus on the issue.

Three times during His ministry, Jesus performed miracles to prove there was life after death. Life was restored to a girl shortly after she died (Matthew 9), to a youth on the way to the cemetery (Luke 7), and a man who had been buried several days (John 11). Jesus' own resurrection was the final proof.

Believers in Corinth thought Jesus was returning in their lifetime, so they were concerned about friends who had died. In a letter, Paul assured them there would be a resurrection:

> In a moment, in the twinkling of an eye, at the last trumpet; for the trumpet will sound, and the dead will be raised imperishable, and we will be changed. (1 Corinthians 15:52)

This future resurrection has been the hope of believers since that time, and seems to be the same one referred to in Revelation:

> Blessed and holy is the one who has a part in the first resurrection; over these the second death has no power, but they will be priests of God and of Christ and will reign with Him for a thousand years. (Revelation 20:6)

Who are these people? Two groups are included, all believers who have died with faith in Christ, and second, all believers alive at the time of His appearing.

This beatitude gives believers assurance of avoiding eternal punishment—the second death. It also gives insight into their purpose during the millennium, the thousand-year period during which Christ reigns. No wonder believers welcome His returning with joy. It is something worth preparing for!

Prayer: Thank You, Lord, for the blessed hope of Your returning. Help us to always be prepared for Your coming.

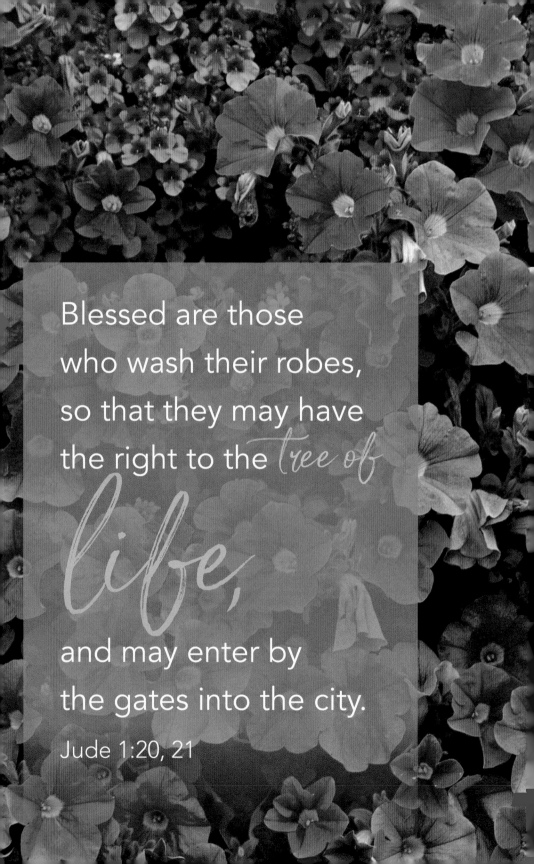

Blessed are those who wash their robes, so that they may have the right to the *tree of* *life,* and may enter by the gates into the city.

Jude 1:20, 21

Entering the City

After describing the judgments coming upon unbelievers, the angel gave John a glimpse of the new heaven and new earth; then he saw the new Jerusalem and gave a graphic description. The beauty of that city is beyond our comprehension. Next the angel shows John a river, and "On either side of the river was the tree of life" (Revelation 22:2). We last read about this tree in Genesis.

As the vision is completed, the messenger adds two final blessings. First, he repeats the blessing that he gave before the vision began:

> And behold, I am coming quickly. Blessed is he who heeds the words of the prophecy of this book. (22:7)

The final blessing also repeats a warning from a previous blessing, another caution to be prepared for Christ's coming:

> Blessed are those who wash their robes, so that they may have the right to the tree of life, and may enter by the gates into the city. (22:14)

The mention of the Tree of Life here shows the unity of the Bible. From Genesis to Revelation, we see man's struggle because of Adam's sin. We also see God's grace working to restore humanity to their original home. The culmination of that struggle is shown here, where the redeemed children of Adam may enter the city and again have access to the Tree of Life.

This second reminder also shows the importance of preparing for Christ's coming. This blessing includes the privileges of entering the city.

The summary of the blessings of Revelation is very clear. Twice we are told to heed the warnings of the book. Twice we are told to be clothed in the righteousness of Christ by faith. When properly prepared, we enter the City and partake of the Tree of Life, then live forever with the Lord.

Prayer: Lord, thank You for this hope; by faith we look forward to eternity with You.

For Further Reading

This book is designed as an introduction to reading through the Bible annually. Hopefully, it will encourage many readers in this practice. Establishing a regular time and place for Bible reading is a good beginning.

Establishing a consistent method of reading is the second step. The traditional method used for many years was three chapters each weekday and four chapters on Sunday to get through the Bible in the year.

Bibles are available specifically designed for daily readings for the year. As technology has advanced, annual Bible readings also are available online.

Continual effort is the final step, accompanied with determination to develop the habit of annual Bible reading. Acheiving the goal will be worth the effort.

Notes

Notes